Hard Truths, Healing Truths:
120 Perspectives to Make Shift Happen in Your Life

By Sharisa T. Robertson

I0192746

Lilies of the Field Media

www.lotfmedia.com

Hard Truths, Healing Truths:
120 Perspectives to Make Shift Happen in Your Life

Hard Truths, Healing Truths: 120 Perspectives to Make Shift Happen in Your Life

Copyright © 2016 by Sharisa T. Robertson

www.sharisarobertson.com

All rights reserved, including the right of reproduction in whole or in any part in any form, without written permission from publisher, except by a reviewer who may quote brief passages in a review; nor may any part of this book be reproduced in any manner whatsoever, stored in a retrieval system, or transmitted in any form or by any means electronic, mechanical, photocopying, recording, or other, without written permission from publisher.

ISBN: 978-0-9854961-3-5

Published by Lilies of the Field Media, LLC, Detroit, MI info@lotfmedia.com

Cover Design:
Editing:
Book Layout: Sharisa T. Robertson

Lilies of the Field Media, LLC and its author hope that you will find encouragement, inspiration, and information within the pages of this book. Happy Reading and welcome to our world!!!!

Presented To:

_____

From: _____

Date: _____

Dedication

This book is dedicated to you the reader. My hope is that you will be inspired to shift your life and experience the success that you've desired, inside than out.

Table of Contents

Moment of Truth: A Message for You 1

#1 3

#2 4

#3 5

#4 6

#5 7

#6 8

#7 9

#8 10

#9 11

#10 12

#11 13

#12 14

#13 15

#14 16

#15 17

#16 18

#17 19

#18 20

#19 21

#20 22

#21 23

#22 24

#23 25

#24 26

#25 27

#26 28

#27 29

#28 30

#29 31

#30 32

#31 33

#32 34
#33 35
#34 36
#35 37
#36 38
#37 39
#38 40
#39 41
#40 42
#41 43
#42 44
#43 45
#44 46
#45 47
#46 48
#47 49
#48 50
#49 51
#50 52
#51 53
#52 54
#53 55
#54 56
#55 57
#56 58
#57 59
#58 60
#59 61
#60 62
#61 63
#62 64
#63 65
#64 66
#65 67

#66 68

#67 69

#68 70

#69 71

#70 72

#71 73

#72 74

#73 75

#74 76

#75 77

#76 78

#77 79

#78 80

#79 81

#80 82

#81 83

#82 84

#83 85

#84 86

#85 87

#86 88

#87 89

#88 90

#89 91

#90 92

#91 93

#92 94

#93 95

#94 96

#95 97

#96 98

#97 99

#98 100

#99 101

#100 102

#101... 103

#102 104

#103 105

#104 106

#105 107

#106 108

#107 109

#108 110

#109 111

#110... 112

#111 113

#112...114

#113 115

#114...116

#115 117

#116...118

#117...119

#118...120

#119 121

#120 122

Acknowledgments 124

About the Author..125

"Ish happens but shift happens, too."

---Sharisa T. Robertson

Moment of Truth: A Message for You

I wanted to put together a book that was not filled with a lot of fluff or long stories, but straight to the point, bit size powerful messages, that if taken to heart would make a huge impact in your life. I love to collect and write quotes that are reminiscent of soul (mind, will, emotions) stimulating moments that connects your well- being (a product of your reality, state of consciousness) with that stir in your spirit. Hard Truths, Healing Truths is this and it meant to alter your emotional and mental perspective about your circustances and yourself.

Do more than just read this book.

Pay attention to which Perspective(s) resonates deep within you, which Perspective(s) offends you, pisses you off, hurts your feelings, and makes you say hmmm, and/or pull at your heartstrings. Those are the one(s) that were written specifically for you at this time and meant for you to read. Don't ignore it, don't blow by it, even if you don't have a full understanding of everything or you've been avoiding it all, take the time, this time to dig into "it."

Now is the time to go forth. Work through your ish but know it is the shift (and where it is taking you and what it is revealing to you) that needs your focus the most. That is where transformation is waiting to occur.

I was inspired by someone who I admire, Akilah Richards, Founder of The Radical Selfie (check her out). She was conducting a webinar about writing your own personal manifesto and one of the steps states to speak your truth. She stated, *to start with a hard truth about yourself and then speak a healing truth. Don't avoid*

1

the tough stuff but don't accept or wallow in it. Put your (healing) truth over your doubt.

Hard Truths, Healing Truths caught my attention and I knew it was the name of this book and way better than the title that I had originally. Even more so the meaning behind it was just as compelling, intriguing, and transcending.

This book does exactly what she says and I want you to look at it as a tool of that nature. A tool that prompts a shift in you by confronting the things you may not realize, that you may be denying, or that may be a bit harsh *but* this book isn't design to keep you there in self-pity or in your troubles, even if you are going through it at this very moment.

My intent is to get into the ugliness and spark the internal fight that will show you the other side of you, a deeper look into your soul, and to activate your willpower to begin the journey to self-discovery and do the work to win within. That victory will overflow externally.

Pain can be turned into purpose.

I know this firsthand because these words that I have written in this book, is for me first, then you, a reminder for us both. I share with you my hard truths and my healing truths that were birthed from my own experiences and struggles, in hopes that you will step out of the lies that you have been told or even embraced as your very own beliefs.

If you are not being uplifted (inside and out) then you are being weighed down. It is time to shed some pounds and make room for the better. The process isn't always pretty but it is necessary.

Hard but Healing, this is your moment of Truth.

Sharisa

#1

*S*tand

in the power of who you were created to be, not in
the pity of who you were conditioned to be.

#2

*A*ddress

the issue without attacking the person.

#3

*C*ontribute

more to the life that you want instead of the life that you don't want.

#4

$\mathcal{H}$appiness

is based on what is happening. Joy is a lifestyle.
There is nothing wrong with being happy, we need
those moments but why not push for joy?

#5

*L*ive

not just survive. Experience, not just exist. Be
enriched, not just want to be rich.

#6

*B*e

audacious enough to promote and demote
some people, things, words, thoughts, and behaviors
in your life.

#7

*D*oing

nothing is still something. Not making a decision is
still deciding. All decisions made or "not made"
comes with a reward/consequence and a
lesson/blessing.

#8

*B*elieve

in the impossible, fall in love with possibility, and
allow God to work through you and use you to make
it a certainty.

#9

*Y*ou
don't have to secretly want what someone else has.
Don't allow beautiful distractions to distract you
from your own potential. You are just as deserving,
so go out and get yours.

#10

*I*nstead

of living a life artificially flavored, trying to appeal
to the masses. Be original,100% natural
and let the masses (those that are real and not fake)
appeal to you.

#11

*C*ommitment

starts you. As you begin to focus and change
yourself, everything and everyone around you will
fall into or out of place accordingly.

#12

*I*f

you keep yourself hydrated and replenished from
the start, you won't constantly search for someone
or something to quench your thirst.

#13

*B*ecome

the love that you seek, beloved.

#14

*S*top

proving yourself right on the things that are so wrong.

#15

*P*eople

in your circle should complement who you already
are and what you already know, value, and love
about yourself. If not, reevaluate them and yourself.

#16

*E*ither
you will conquer it or you will be condemned by it.

#17

*C*reate

a life worth living and a life worth dying for.

#18

*L*et

the world know how great you are, not by telling them but by showing them. It is not your talk that helps and inspires people, it's your walk. Make sure that they both align.

#19

*T*here
are no returns on empty "investments." You'll always come out broke and broken. Invest your time, energy and love
wisely.

#20

*T*he
one person you can't escape, divorce, or avoid is
yourself.

#21

A

victim mentality attracts victimization but not at the hands of "them," at the hands of you.

#22

How

much do you have to endure before you decide to let go? Whatever you hold on to with tightly closed fist, will eventually hold on even tighter to you.

#23

*D*on't

talk yourself out of your common sense today.

#24

*I*t

is one thing to identify with your past and it is another to allow your past to be your identity.

#25

*D*isable

your enabling and watch how quick those that act as
if they are unable become able.

#26

You can't expect someone who still hasn't healed to help you heal from what they have done to you. Hold them accountable but know you are responsible for your own healing.

#27

What

effect are you having on people? Are you affecting them with your love and positivity or are you infecting them with your hate and negativity?

#28

*S*ometimes

forgiveness means letting go of the pain but holding
on to the person and most times it is letting go of
the pain and letting go of the person too.

#29

*T*hings

tend to happen in life not to stop you but to prepare you for what's to come so that you will become unstoppable.

#30

Know

the difference between taking a chance
and settling for less.

#31

*S*top

allowing your childhood pains to block
your adulthood blessings.

#32

*Y*our
need to heal has to be just as much as
your need to breathe.

#33

Vow

to no longer live a life that validates your victimization but more so validates your victory.

#34

Don't

mistake barriers for limitations. What may block your path doesn't mean it has to stop you on your path. Deal with it, detour around or over it, push through it, and learn from it.

#35

You

might be hindered but you are not defeated.

#36

Who

makes the decisions in your life? You or fear?

#37

*B*eing
resistant in your process will cause you to renege on
your purpose.

#38

*T*each

others how to treat you by not allowing them to
mistreat you.

#39

Having

the strength to lie to yourself and others, shouldn't
be the only thing strong about you.

#40

*I*t's

bad when others think and speak ill of you, but it is
worse when you think, speak, and believe those
things about yourself and become them.

#41

A

true relationship with another should not come at the expense of your dignity, sanity, peace of mind, or self respect. If it does, then you are not in a real (healthy) relationship with them, nor yourself.

#42

*L*ead

from the lesson and not from the pain.

#43

You
are not a doormat, stop allowing them to walk all over you. You are not a garbage can, stop allowing them to dump their trash on you. You are not a punching bag, stop allowing them to beat up on you.

#44

*C*hange

for the better not bitter.

#45

*T*rue

loyalty to others will never require or demand you
to be disloyal to yourself.

#46

*S*urrender

to your past or surrender *your* past.

#47

Don't

cry and then give up. Cry and keep going.

#48

*C*ompromise

and even a certain level of sacrifice should not put you in harm's way (mentally, emotionally, physically, financially, and spiritually).

#49

*S*top

building walls start building bridges.

#50

*N*o

longer dwell on your mistakes. You own them and try your best not to repeat them again.

#51

*D*efine

your own success and know that you can and will be
successful in all that you do.

#52

*D*o

the work to make your reality look like your dreams.

#53

*F*ool
you once, shame on them. Fool you twice, shame on you. Fool you three times or more, and you are a volunteer to the foolishness. And that is the real shame.

#54

Don't

let the dysfunction from your past become the way
that you function in your present.

#55

*Y*ou
have to go through it in order to grow and
get through it.

#56

*S*tarting

over is not failure. Not starting over or trying to make something be that can never be is not only failure but it is torture.

#57

When
you are you, you don't have to pretend, you just have to be.

#58

W hat
appears to be the end, is actually a new beginning.

#59

*T*o

practice patience is to deter your want for instant gratification as you pursue your need for lifelong satisfaction.

#60

*B*e

you freely, creatively, lovingly, resiliently, joyously, courageously, purposely.

#61

*J*ust
because it is convenient for you now doesn't mean
it won't be an inconvenience for you later. Be
sagacious in your decisions, now and later.

#62

A

peace of mind may be the piece of life that you are missing.

#63

*L*ife

is knowing how to stop and smell the roses but
being careful not to get stung by a bee.

#64

T̥o be down for the cause you have to be up for the challenge.

#65

W hen

you have nothing to lose, you gain everything and win.

#66

*N*aw,

you're not acting all brand new, you've just been renewed.

#67

You can only change yourself and it's your change that will inspire change around you.

#68

*S*tep

outside and smile at sun. In return, as
acknowledgement of your existence, the sun will
kiss you with its rays. So shine, be shined upon,
enjoy and bask in it.

#69

*B*reak

free from the walking dead and choose to live life.

#70

*F*ree
yourself from the business of others and mind your
own.

#71

While

trying to find out what life has to give to you, figure
out what you have to give to life.

#72

*S*truggle

is success not yet achieved.

#73

D.

what resonates with your spirit not with what
appeases your (or their) ego.

#74

*N*o

makes room for yes.

#75

*T*here's

a distinction between managing your emotions so
you can suppress and control them and getting to
the root of your emotions so you can understand
and heal them.

#76

*B*ecome

the you that you dream of.

#77

*E*verything

leaves clues if you pay attention. Know which ones to follow and which ones to stay away from.

#78

*C*hoose

your fights wisely and be strategic according to the situation. Make sure you're not winning the battle but losing the war.

#79

*R*elease

so that you can receive.

#80

*L*abel

your bags and decide if they are worth carrying.

#81

You don't need to seek permission to be you. But you do need to give yourself permission to find out who you are and to become who you are meant to be.

#82

You
may not have the same opportunities as others but
if you have more drive than others, you can create
your own opportunities.

#83

*Y*our

worst experiences are your best teachers.

#84

*F*orgiveness

is your F-you to the person or/and situation as you gain your sense of freedom and move on. It is not acceptance, trust, or reconciliation *unless* you choose it to be so.

#85

Stand

up on your 2 feet and live. Or keep crawling on your knees trying to survive.

#86

*D*on't
get stuck at just wanting and hoping for it. Do the
work to manifest it.

#87

*I*t

doesn't need to be revived, if it was killing you.

#88

*G*ratitude

does wonders for your attitude.

#89

*P*ursuing

what keeps you temporarily content, will make you
miss out on what will keep you permanently
fulfilled.

#90

You

cannot heal a hurt from the same level of consciousnessin which it was created in.

#91

W hen

your vision is beyond sight don't be deterred by what you see ahead of you stay focus on what you focus and on path.

#92

*S*uccess,

happiness, relaxation, freedom, creativity, healing, peace of mind, even pain, doesn't look the same to everybody. However, you show up in the world, focus on being you.

#93

*E*veryday

you are creating your legacy so create everyday purposefully.

#94

*M*aking

the wrong decisions makes it easy to find trouble in
all the right places.

#95

*D*on't
mistake emotional resistance for emotional resilience.

#96

*F*ind
the positive in what appears to be negative.

#97

*F*ear
will have you running from nothing and hiding from
something. So just face it.

#98

*R*eflect

Inwardly before projecting outwardly.

#99

*G*et
quiet. Silence has a way of helping you get loud and clear on things.

#100

*Y*ou

can be present and absent at the same time.

#101

*S*tuck?

It isn't just because what is going outside of
you. It is also because what is going on inside
of you.

#102

$y$ou
can think you're deserving of something and at the
same time don' feel worthy of it.

#103

*F*eelings
are your indicators of your energy not your enemy.
What are your emotions trying to tell you about
you?

#104

Self - care

heals self - abuse.

#105

*D*on't

become so educated that you cannot not think.

#106

*L*ove

your life and your life will love you back.

#107

*B*eing

use to a thing doesn't make it useful. Let go of trying to find use in what is now useless.

#108

*P*rogress

includes a process.

#109

*I*t

is never worth having to do wrong by yourself just
to do right by someone else.

#110

*L*et

your next yes propel you into your next best move.
Let your next no propel you into your next best
move.

#111

*N*ever

deprive yourself of rest and of laughter. Your body, soul and spirit needs it.

#112

*Y*our
best version of yourself is a decision away.

#113

*E*verything

won't be a love story but it can be an I learned story, instead.

#114

Maybe

the issue is not that you care too much about what people think of you. Maybe the deeper issue is that you don't care more about yourself to be/become comfortable in your own skin. Maybe it is your judgment of yourself first that is stopping you feeling/thinking highly of yourself.

#115

*Y*ou

know you're beautiful but do you know you're
worthy? Stop exploiting or allowing others to exploit
your beauty. Nothing's wrong with being confident
in your outer appearances but it is detrimental to
use it as a crutch and ignore the other aspects of
yourself. Feel as good as you look.

#116

*S*tay

true to honoring yourself. It is worth the perceived
risk of losing anything or anyone who compromises
who you are, what you stand for, and what you are
working to achieve and become.

#117

*L*et

your capacity (money, talent, ideas)
match your capabilities (time, effort, commitment,
love, space, patience).

#118

*D*on't
be more familiar to drama but a stranger to growth.

#119

*P*retending

to be who you are not isn't the same as preparing to become who you essentially already are. One is just perpetrating a lifestyle. The other is being purposeful in living.

#120

*A*ppreciate

the person who greets you in the mirror every day.

I appreciate you!

*Thank you for purchasing
and reading.
Please leave a review of Amazon!*

Acknowledgments

I am thankful because this is me in a book, a written portrait of my thoughts and self. I am a word girl, feelings girl, and perspective girl and I think this embodies all of that and more.

I am thankful to God for the creative downloads,insights, and wordplay that I am given and having the sense to document them.

I thank my family and friends as always.

I thank you for your support.

About the Author

Sharisa T. Robertson uses her platform as a means to address touchy, taboo, and traumatic topics. She has turned her pain into her purpose by showing others how to do the same by changing their emotional and mental perspective of themselves and their circumstances while also using writing as a tool for healing, release, expression, discovery, and freedom.

Sharisa is the founder, publisher, and author of Lilies of the Field Media, LLC. She is the visionary of 2 books collaborations, A Letter To My Mother: A Daughter's Perspective and A Letter To My Bully: Stick, Stones, and Words Do Hurt. She is a contributing writer to Cheers To Success: Women on the Rise and Owning their Destiny. She is also working on her 3 rd book collab, A Letter To My Abuser and a collection of short stories, her first fiction book.

Writing since she was 10, Sharisa had over 100 episodes of her own TV show written and all on her paper, making her room a fire hazard. After constantly hearing about the starving artist, she made up her mind that it would be impossible to try and actually pursue a career in writing. Although she still wrote in her journal, love to take notes, write in her calendar her passion for writing was pushed aside and she gave it up, only writing on occasion. So to be an author and a business woman over 20 years later, is a dream come true.

www.sharisarobertson.com

www.ingramcontent.com/pod-product-compliance
Lightning Source LLC
Chambersburg PA
CBHW031321040426
42443CB00005B/172